Frank Vervoort

Premium
Version

POLITICS
The Real Face of Our Leaders

Table of Contents

Introduction

I want to thank you and congratulate you for buying the book, "Politics: The Real Face of Our Leaders."

Politics comes innocently enough from the Greek word "polis "which has been defined as "affairs of the cities." When Aristotle wrote his book, *Politics*, around the 4th century, B.C., he described the tendencies and proclivities of men in trying to co-exist with others in the Athenian communities of his Ancient Greece. The eight-volume work was exhaustive in defining the components of groups of erstwhile strangers who decide to peacefully co-exist under a set of agreed-upon rules.

This book provides a sweeping introduction to the world of this "affairs of men and state," especially as it relates to politics in the United States. U.S. politics is at a pretty interesting stage today, what with calls to impeach the sitting U.S. president, and the daily detonation of explosive allegations and charges between the members of opposing political parties.

In Chapters 1 to 3, I provide an introduction to politics and the events and historical milestones that preceded today's political scene in the U.S. We will define politics in the context of human history in the context of politics. Much of Chapters 2 and 3 will examine the political economy of the United States, a country that was founded on gritty commercial and capitalistic endeavors.

In Chapters 4 and 5, the lengthiest chapters, we discuss the current political environment focusing on the United States. We examine the two major political parties in the U.S. the Democrats and Republicans, and the political ideologies and issues that not only define the parties, but drive the political discussion and activism of those who involve themselves in the political process.

Chapters 6 and 7 get into the heart of putting a face into who or what politicians are, where they come from and why they even get into politics in the first place.

Chapter 8 provides an explanation as to the disparity in views on American politics among Americans and those outside America. I describe how the U.S. is unique not only in how it was formed, but how its governance was defined by its founders.

I trust that this book will not only significantly add to your knowledge of politics, but also inspire you to get yourself involved in what is an integral part of civics and participation in the country's political process.

Thanks again for downloading this book, I hope you enjoy it!

Chapter One: Politics on Fire

Politics has not been the same since Republican Donald J. Trump became the 46th President of the United States. Not since the tempestuous Civil War era has there been so much divisiveness, vitriol, and rancor between opposing political parties. Trump has been "running" against his enemies ever since he announced his candidacy in 2015, and his clashes not only with political adversaries but especially the established media, grows everyday as he continues to pummel them with putdowns and insults. No president in recent memory has been subject to calls for impeachment by the opposing political party so early in his term. He was called out as an illegitimate president even before his inauguration, with his political enemies even plotting to sabotage his inauguration festivities with violent protests and attacks. He has been insulted and called names and he has insulted and name-called right back.

The *New York Times*, a bitter Trump critic, tracks the insults that Trump has dished out to his critics and political foes and has chronicled over five hundred of them through the end of 2018. He has among other things called political opponent and critics crazy, fake, low-life, and cry-babies. His enemies of course have not backed down. Jettisoning the long-held tradition of not fully saying the "f" word or its derivatives in addressing political enemies, Rep. Rashida Tlaib, a Democratic congressman from Michigan, called out Trump and told a cheering audience in January, 2019 that they were going to "impeach the motherfucker."

Discarding all decorum among heads of state and former heads of state, Kim Campbell, the former Prime Minister of Canada, called Trump a "Motherf***er" in a tweet a couple of days later.

Most would think that these displays of lack of decorum by educated and civilized people is a sign that politics has hit rock-bottom, and that Donald Trump is the major cause for the coarsening of the political atmosphere in the United States. These incidents and tone however, would be like a Sunday church social compared to incidents going back to the formation of the U.S. as a nation. Verbal jousting was common as it is today, and many conflicts were physical, and even fatal.

<u>Notable political confrontations</u>

In 1777 Button Gwinnett, a signer of the Declaration of Independence, was shot to death in a duel with Lachlan Macintosh who was ironically an American Revolutionary war hero. Their feud was about who was going to have control of command of armed forces in Georgia. The incident happened less than a year after the Declaration of Independence was signed.

In 1804 in the most famous political skirmish in American history, Vice-President (to Thomas Jefferson) Aaron Burr killed Secretary of the Treasury Alexander Hamilton, who Burr believed bad-mouthed him, which led to his loss as Governor of New York. Burr had decided to run for the "lesser" office of governor when it became apparent that Jefferson would not make Burr his running mate in the 1804 elections. Hamilton had floated the idea that Burr was considering pushing New York to secession, and Burr considered Hamilton's actions to have led to his electoral loss.

The American Civil War was the result of the most contentious differences in political philosophy in American history: Slavery. Debating as to whether a person should be considered a human being or a beast of burden was being weighed against the economic survival of many states in the Southern United States. Those pushing for the banning of slavery, the "abolitionists" believed that they were on solid, moral footing. Those that defended slavery pointed out that it was still very much part of global commerce and continuing the practice was essential for the economic future of the people that were engaged in it. It was no surprise that a lot of verbal fireworks ensued in legislative proceedings when American lawmakers debated the thorny issue of slavery. It was an issue that would fracture a nation at the cost of millions of lives.

In May 1854 the Republican senator Charles Sumner from Massachusetts, severely criticized a bill authored by Stephen A. Douglas of Illinois and Andrew Butler of South Carolina. Sumner believed the bill would make slavery even more rampant while the Senate was debating whether to admit more states into the Union. Stung by attacks on his cousin Butler, South Carolina Democratic congressman Preston Brooks decided to do something about it.

A couple of days after Sumner's speech, Brooks entered the Senate chambers, voiced his displeasure at Sumner's allegations and struck the elderly Sumner several times over the head with a cane as Sumner was about to stand up. To discourage anyone from helping Sumner, another Democrat Lawrence Keitt, took out a pistol and prevented anyone from intervening in the beating. Brooks only stopped trashing Sumner when his cane broke after which he and Keitt calmly walked out of the chambers. Sumner survived the horrific attack but the brain damage he sustained would torment him for the rest of his life.

While abolitionists roundly condemned the attack, Southerners celebrated Brooks' actions and described what he did was "socially justifiable."

Less than four years later, the fires that inflamed the hearts and minds of abolitionists and pro-slavery advocates grew even larger. In what is still the biggest brawl in U.S. legislative history, over thirty members of the U.S. House of Representatives skirmished in the Capitol after a contentious debate regarding slavery in the Kansas territory in February, 1858. After an all-night debate, many of the members, tired and frustrated, began to snipe at each other. At just before two in the morning, Keitt once again got involved. He exchanged insults with abolitionist Pennsylvania Republican Galusha Grow and soon began exchanging blows. In a matter of seconds, over thirty other house members joined in the melee. Free Soilers representing a short-lived political movement whose only objective was to prevent slavery from creeping into the Western territories, closed ranks with Northern Republicans and skirmished with Southern Democrats.

Despite the unprecedented scale of the skirmish, it happily dissolved into a chorus of jeers and laughs. While there were no serious injuries, the melee symbolized the deep ideological fissure dividing the country because of the slavery issue: Nothing could be agreed upon through serious legislative debate and very little common ground could be achieved by opposing sides. The nervous laughter and cheers that ended the fracas in the morning would be one of the very few light moments before the country was embroiled in a bloody and bitter war with itself.

Just over a year later, in September, 1859 and less than two years before the start of the Civil War, David C. Broderick, a Senator from California was killed in a duel with a former friend David S. Terry. Terry was the former Chief Justice of the California Supreme Court. Their feud was about whether slavery should be abolished. Broderick, a "Free Soiler," was an outspoken critic of slavery. Terry blamed Broderick for losing an election as Broderick pounded on Terry's pro-slavery views.

All these violent episodes were a result of someone passionately defending a belief or an issue with conviction. Those who brawled and died believed that it was worth a mortal battle to preserve their dignity while defending their beliefs.

They debated and skirmished about politics - a passion that has burned intensely in the hearts and minds of human beings from the very beginning.

Chapter Two: The Origin and Nature of Politics

Ever since Homo sapiens emerged from their hunting and gathering ways and pooled themselves into communities, politics became an essential part of the community of men. Politics was not a past time or a form of entertainment as it is viewed by many today. It was a set of activities that was crucial so that men could live among themselves harmoniously. They created and lived within a set of unwritten rules and laws that described what they could and could not do in their community.

<u>Leadership and selection</u>

From the earliest times, all communities of men selected a leader or group of leaders among themselves who they felt had the toolkit and intelligence to lead them. In the earliest human settlements, the strongest and to the communities' assessment, wisest of their groups were selected to lead them. At first it was a matter of who could physically defend their groups the best and who could best help secure food and supplies. Over time, more emphasis was placed on a man who projected the most "wisdom" and knowledge to help navigate the communities through increasingly complex issues and situations.

With small groups, it was fairly easy to get consensus among a small number of people and a limited number of situations (food, shelter, defense from predators) as to who was the right person or persons to lead them. A show of hands or nods of assent was all that was required to agree on the leader.

Bigger communities burgeoned into fiefdoms and kingdoms, and leader selection was sometimes done through force. A king or a lord or a village chief would could simply banish or even kill a competitor for the leadership role. In the Bible, especially the Old Testament, kings and leaders often obtained their position through force and even treachery. It is still the way of life in many remote tribes in the world, and once in a while, a violent takeover or coup de 'etat is planned and carried out by an opposing faction as what happened in Gabon as recently as January 2019.

In the past two hundred years or so, most countries have settled down as peaceful democracies and have devised ways to develop systematic procedures to choose a leader. A significant majority of countries utilize elections with the attendant campaigns, candidate selection, and voting. Occasionally, a precious few leaders have simply grabbed power through intimidation, treachery, cheating, and even murder, mostly in the name of grabbing a king's ransom of a country's resources.

<u>Resources and property – Political economy</u>

A very important aspect of politics is economics, which has taken a larger share of the attention of politicians. As human history has progressed, leaders have been entrusted with increasingly huge amounts of the resources available to a particular group of people. Among the first humans, food and supplies that they gathered and stored comprised most of the resources that the community had to take care of. It was then up to the leaders to figure out how these resources are used and distributed. Today, politicians are tasked to be custodians and judicious distributors of collectively hundreds of trillions of dollars of resources.   Leaders have to negotiate what to spend or even not to spend at all, and they have to justify to their constituents on national and local levels on why they need to obtain some resources and explain why they were not able to secure needed ones.   While a vast majority are proficient in managing resources, not all of them cannot be trusted to do the right things.

Corrupt kings and dictators have been ripping off entire countries that they rule since the beginning of recorded history.   Countries pillaged by leaders that their own citizens placed in power have sometimes done more damage than if marauders from other countries had done the pillaging.   They indiscriminately flaunted their own laws that were made to protect its citizens from the very people like them.

<u>Laws, religion and punishment</u>

A key aspect of politics is the creation of laws and systems of punishment for citizens who violated those laws.   The first written law that was not based on religion was the *Hammurabi* in ancient Babylon.   These were laws that were promulgated by the political leaders of time, but were limited to Babylon's citizens.

After the *Hammurabi*, many laws that governed some countries were based on religion.   In the Middle East, the first pervasive set of laws that were applied to a large swathe of people were the Mosaic laws of the pre-Christian Jews.   The prophet Moses was actually a political leader because he had the responsibility to lead hundreds of thousands of people in a treacherous journey in their escape from Egypt.   The laws that Moses are said to have come from God in Mount Sinai covered worship behavior and moral codes, and became the basis of the so-called Levitical laws (chronicled in the Old Testament book Leviticus) that covered a broad set of rules governing individual behavior.   These were eventually codified in the *Torah*, the first five books of the Holy Bible.

Mosaic law is among the first set of political rules that prescribed capital punishment for violating laws. Adultery and idolatry were among the dozen or so infractions that warranted the death penalty.   Death was carried out by stoning, after which the body of the dead person was hung up on a stake or wall for others to see – presumably a deterrent from committing the same crimes.

Until they were overrun by foreigners like the Romans Jewish religious law governed daily life, and the "politicians" that enforced them were priests such as the Sanhedrin. Religion, law and politics were merged for thousands of years before the establishment of Western democracies. Islam spread to many countries beginning in the sixth century A.D. as the Quran became the handbook for daily living and punishment in the countries that fell under the Moslems.

The Greeks, via the teachings of Aristotle and other philosophers had the political profile of their cities adequately mapped out and defined.   Roman law was somewhat patterned after Greek law: a non-religious set of laws that governed most of the world for over a thousand years beginning in the 4th Century, B.C.   These became among the first written sets of laws that politicians created, pre-dating the British *Magna Carta* and was the first set of laws to define and differentiate the functions of citizens, its legislators, and its judicial branch, a pre-cursor to the separation of powers doctrines that govern many nations today.

In Middle-Age Europe, monarchies controlled the governance of their countries, and laws and punishment were arbitrary and much of their application was based on political patronage which depended on how "close" you were to the throne. A political layer below these monarchies were lords and masters who were part of the feudal society. Each lord had dominion over a particular patch of land and ruled serfs and farmers in the manner of a tight-fisted king. This was the hallmark of the feudal society that was the prevailing political model of the times.

The political fires in Europe then began to get stoked as unrest bubbled from a growing political underclass that began to resent the abuses by the monarchies. The kings were overtaxing their citizens to fund their lavish lifestyles and ill-advised foreign adventures. Revolts and wars like the French Revolution led to creation of democracies and representative forms of governments with democratically elected political heads. This form of government is the most commonplace today. Many historians believe that the leaders of the revolutionary movements where inspired by the American revolution in 1776 which is discussed in more detail in Chapter 3.

After the 18th century, most Western nations had written laws in place that defined the nature of politics in their own. Written constitutions were drafted by leaders who selected democratically among a group of qualified candidates, and all that was left was for the citizens to conduct their normal business within the purview of laws meant to protect themselves and their nations.

<u>Relationships with other communities – International politics</u>

An important function of politicians is the nurturing of relationships with other sovereign and foreign nations. While countries can theoretically exist on their own, international commerce and diplomacy is necessary to sustain a political unit. Nations will need everything from food, raw materials, manufactured goods, and even labor to supplement what they have within their borders. The head of a nation must have the political skills to extract the most favorable terms with diplomacy, good negotiating skills, persuasiveness, and even the threat of force, if necessary

With regards to force, a political leader is usually also charged with the national defense of a nation. Under a cloud of war or attacks on their countries, political leaders need to thread the fine line between capitulation and the use of force in a defensive and even offensive manner. One of the biggest political challenges for any leader is to harness their citizens' will to provide moral and material support in case a nation has to go to war.

Military success and national defense (or offense for that matter) has defined many a leader and in a young America it was crucial to its birth and survival.

Chapter Three: American Politics and Politicians Before the Current Era

If you are a diehard political junkie and stepped into a time machine to go back one hundred fifty years in the U.S., the most glaring difference would be between that of Republicans and Democrats. In the 19th century, Republicans were considered the heroes of black folk as they endured and tried to flee slavery. The Southern States on the other hand, were represented mostly by Democrats who wanted to keep the slavery status quo to keep their economic machinery running. A lot has changed since then and taking another trip back one hundred fifty years will even bring more surprises and revelations.

"We hate kings"

Many call it myth or folklore, and others say there is a tendency to romanticize the motives of why Europeans first settled in what is now the United States. The easy answers are that Europeans settled in North America beginning in the late 17th century for three sometimes intersecting reasons.

First, some were said to avoid religious persecution especially in England who beginning in the 16th century, began to merge religion and affairs of the state, an absolute monarchy with a single king in charge.

Second, many were very much threatened by the rule of European kings who were arbitrary and uneven in their treatment of their subjects. There was a lot of patronage and individual freedoms were often curtailed and even violated if subjects had to political influence and had connections to the monarchs.

Third, the choking rule of the kings encroached on the free exercise of commerce, especially those involving foreign goods. Money and riches were still very much in the minds of enterprising people and many felt that they would rather face the uncertainties of uncharted territory than stay home in Europe and deal with the whims of the monarchs.

Most of those who left Europe to stake their life in the uncertain new world departed because of disgust with their monarchs. Politics was the last thing on their minds when they descended from their boats into an uncertain future in the New World. What they were certain of is that they were permanently fleeing the distasteful monarchial politics in their old countries. Little did they know that they were about to soon to be at the forefront of a global political upheaval although it would take over a hundred years to do so.

A new type of democracy

The European settlers who arrived in what is now North America unwittingly found themselves living in communities not unlike the first organized communities of homo sapiens thousands of years before them. They found themselves in new and uncharted land, with no immediate food sources, predators, and hostile indigenous tribes who were intent on either driving them away, stealing from them, or just plain hurting them for sport. They were still European (mostly

British) subjects who worked hard to apply their Old World knowledge and traditions to a completely unknown and hostile world. This was the trade-off for their fleeing the oppressive clutches of their former lands: While they were still European citizens, they were also politically emancipated persons who could live their lives with less oversight and duress from oppressive governments.

These "colonists" as they were called, did an excellent job in resettling in the New World given all the odds and disadvantage. Many of them died because of exposure and hostile attacks from the indigenous Americans, and their persistence led to the creation of the formidable nation that the U.S. is today. They were able to create informal political systems within small colonist villages and eventually the growing numbers of colonists from Europe overrun the New World as new arrivals took advantage of the knowledge and experience of those who came before them.

They are commonly known today as "Pilgrims". Today's schools portray them as bitter white people leaving the comforts of Europe in the 1600's to claim an unknown land as their own; land they will soon steal as "settlers" from indigenous Indians. They would top off the merciless takeover by ruthlessly hauling slaves from Africa to do their greedy capitalistic bidding. But enough of K-12 textbook content.

The truth is that the "first Americans" were socialists, federalists, religious fanatics, Quakers, Shakers and candlestick makers. Starting in the early seventeenth century, the motley crews of everyday men joined a multitude of other wayfarers with varying ideologies, nationalities and religions as they abandoned Europe and made their way across the Atlantic to the sprawling, unknown wilderness of North America. They were lured by only the promise of new possibilities and the free exercise of their chosen faiths and lifestyles. Hungry for an existence that until then had only dreamed about, they embarked on a mortal gamble with the highest stakes in play: their very lives and those of their loved ones.

These early "immigrants" liberated themselves not only from oppressive governments but also from the limitations imposed them by cultures, societies and the attitudes of the age. Imagination, persistence, audacity, and exceptionalism would be the heart and soul of their liberation. This first wave of immigrants to North America typified the qualities of "classic liberalism" that was the spirit behind the creation of a United States of America. Disparate personalities and beliefs from across the oceans came together; linked only with the belief that liberty and industry were the necessary requirements for success and advancement. The early settlers understood that personal liberty, one derived from a Divine Providence; a Creator that could make possible the economic and political liberties that would transform these seemingly unrelated groups into the greatest nation on earth.

In less than 100 years from the first arrivals in the 1600's, the New World had enough flourishing colonists who had succeeded economically beyond anyone's wildest prediction. Because of this Britain was compelled to impose a new version of its monarchial rule on its New World subjects. The colonists were put under the watchful eye of British governors who required the colonists to remit taxes to the England. The British government sent troops and commissioned home-grown officers to assist the British forces and the appointed governors to oversee the colonists' activities. One of these home-grown officers was an educated gentleman from Virginia, George Washington. Washington eventually earned the rank of colonel despite a less than stellar military career.

<u>The King messes up again and a new political order is born</u>

The colonists' successes were a boon to England's coffers and the seemingly endless string of economic successes seemed like a never-ending source of funding for the Crown. Over time however, England succeeded in alienating its subjects by subjecting them to ever-increasing regulations and taxes.   In 1774, representatives from the colonies organized themselves politically into the Massachusetts Provincial Congress, which was to be the governing body of a nation-in-progress.   The Congress included the so-called Founding Fathers such as John Hancock and Samuel Adams. The Congress appointed George Washington as the commanding officer of its continental army, largely comprised of untrained conscripts who the British initially scoffed at.

The colonial rebels were written off early as sure losers by the British and many foreign observers. But they held on brilliantly and actually sparked uprisings in Europe by common folk against monarchs and their elites.   The victory by the colonies and its undermanned and underequipped amateurs over the professionally-trained British army is the stuff of legends. The colonies officially earned their sovereign nation status when the Treaty of Paris was signed in 1783 and with it the need to establish a new form of government and establish a new nation.

 Defeating the British was one thing, but there was a bigger job at hand: Building a nation from scratch, an altogether much more daunting task.

<u>The new nation faces harsh political realities</u>

The United States set itself up initially as a political unit comprised of the thirteen original colonies. The colonies were originally grouped into four territories. The Southern colonies were comprised of (North and South) Carolina, Virginia, Georgia, and Georgia. The Middle Colonies were made up of Delaware, Pennsylvania, New Jersey, and New York.   The New England colonies was comprised of Connecticut, Rhode Island, Massachusetts, and New Hampshire. The founders of the new nation immediately began the process of creating a new nation by drafting and passing the Articles of Confederation, a document which most considered wanting but they eventually crafted what to many was a perfect document and convened in Philadelphia to draft it: the U.S. Constitution.   They quickly appended it with The Bill of Rights and the colonies began its new life as independent and free United States. The Continental Congress did not elect a president until the country was set up with the ratification of the U.S. Constitution in 1788 and George Washington was inaugurated as the country's first president in 1789.

The U.S. Constitution was a unique document that explicitly defined the political institutions and mechanisms of an emerging nation.   But the overarching theme in the discussions in the formation of the new country was how a "national" government was going to function in the United States.   After some impassioned debate, the Founding Fathers determined that the national government of their new country would be as different as possible from the England that they knew and learned to despise.

First, the did not want a "king" or a similar facsimile of one to run their country. Second, they did not want any part of government to have any edge in influence over any other part. The separation of powers doctrine therefor was an integral part of the Constitution: The executive, legislative, and judicial branches would influence on how the country was run, but each branch's influence would be tempered by the other two. Third, they wanted the individual states not to be subservient to the national government whose principal functions would mostly be national defense and maintenance of common assets. The lawmaking out of the way, they marched on the business of running a new nation.

Even the country's way of voting for its president reflected the need for each state to have a voice in the outcome of any presidential elections. Unlike every other election system in the world that determines the winner by counting the popular votes, the United States utilizes the electoral college system where each state is given a relatively fixed number of votes based on the number of its congressional districts instead of its population. While the number of electoral votes is still roughly in proportion to a state's population, there have been instances where the winner of the presidential election had significantly less votes than the loser as in the recent cases in 2016 and 2000. The electoral college system was designed so that one state could not "overwhelm" another state in terms of its "voice" in deciding who will lead the nation.

<u>The first thirty years</u>

From a political standpoint, the first quarter of a century of the United State was not marked by any serious differences of opinion by its lawmakers. The country's major problem was fending off attacks from within and without the country. The indigenous Americans continued to plague the foreign white people who were increasingly nudging them off their traditional stomping grounds. And then there was the British who sensed that the new United States was still fragile and vulnerable for re-conquest. In 1812, they tried to overwhelm the U.S. armies with plans of re-taking some territory but were once again defeated by the determined Americans. Finally free of the biggest foreign threat the United States, the country's leaders finally could concentrate on building their nation. They were able to revive the country's economic engine with the same vigor as before the Revolutionary War. Transportation infrastructure was built at an impressive pace, colleges sprouted up everywhere, and the country quickly began to have all the features associated with a self-sustaining sovereign nation. Hard work and imagination ignited a dizzying pace of economic activity which helped finance the new country's growth. Alexander de Tocqueville, the French historian gave the first formal exhaustive report on his observations on the growing world power that was fast becoming the United States. In Democracy in America, de Tocqueville observed that adherence to religious faith, strong local politics, respect for the law, and a fierce determination to protect itself were the driving forces the young country's surge to the pinnacle of national and world power. De Tocqueville's observations were made just over fifty years after the founding American colonists declared themselves "free" from Britain with the Declaration of Independence.

A major factor in this economic revival was the introduction of an efficient and cheap source of productivity: slave labor.

<u>Money or morality?</u>

Slavery had been a practice worldwide since men began invading each other's territories. In the case of the United States, colonists already owned slaves over a hundred years before the Revolutionary War and the birth of the nation. The selling and transporting of slaves was a lucrative business especially in Europe. The slave traders got most of their "inventory" by raiding villages in Africa and hauling off men, women, and boys and transporting them to the New World. The biggest number of African slaves landed the Caribbean and Central and South America and just under 400,000 of over ten million slaves made it to what is now the U.S. In those dark years, African slaves were considered as chattel and not human and were often treated with less care and respect than dogs and other domestic animals.

In North America, slave labor was an important and cost-effective production tool. For practically no compensation except the barest of accommodations and food, the slaves could be be counted upon to provide over 12 to 16 hours of work every day seeding and harvesting cotton, tobacco, and other crops in the South. Before the Revolutionary War, there was no political fallout from the practice because the colonies were effectively a British province and as long as the South generated enough profits and the remittances and taxes to England, nobody really cared about the welfare of the blacks.

When the British were subdued and the United States was formed however, a big part of the country, especially in the North, felt that slave labor was not consistent with the principles of independence that the Founding Fathers founded the new nation on. If it was indeed a country of free men for free men, why did it have men within its boundaries who were only not free, but were treated with less compassion and care than beasts of burden? The South countered with the argument that even the original U.S. Constitution counted slaves as one-third human and therefore not eligible to vote. They also contended that there were no laws that outlawed slavery so there was no legal barrier to their continued existence.

The political debate about whether to keep slavery in the United States began when many Northern states abolished slavery by 1805. The invention of the cotton gin however, required ever increasing amounts of slave labor and at least maintaining the current levels. In 1808, the importation of slaves was banned but the Southern slave owners had ways of maintaining their slave population. Their existing slaves were "bred" to provide offspring for future work, but the biggest source of new slaves was the smuggling of slaves from Central and South America via what is today Florida, which was not yet fully a part of the United States. Because economics was the lifeblood of the nation, the political forces behind keeping slavery cited income and monetary gains. Its opponents cited morality and adherence to the country's founding principles. Morality vs. Money continues to be a common thread of discussion in U.S. politics to the present day, but in the 19th century, the debate meant the difference between monetary ruin and survival. For millions, it would soon be a life and death situation.

<u>The country turns on itself – the failure of politics</u>

A compromise over slavery at hindsight seemed doomed from the start. One side of the political fence, the Republicans had a moral argument that they wanted to ram down the gullets of the intractable Democrats who overwhelmingly came from the South. The Democrats' political position was one based on money and economics, and they tried to convince the Republicans that it would be immoral to deprive Southerners of income and industry. The Republicans represented the North whose people were making money from non-agricultural trade and commerce and agriculture contributed very little to their economy. Democrats were indignant that not only were the Republicans forcing a way of thinking on them, they were also trying to deprive the South of their way to earn a living while Northerners happily went about their daily lives earning money their way.

It was in this poisonous atmosphere that that Republican Abraham Lincoln stepped in as president of an increasingly divided country. The lawyer from Illinois an abolitionist state, took his residence at the White House in Northeast Washington D.C., surrounded by states that were staunchly anti-slavery. But even as he defeated the Southern Democrat John Breckenridge in an electoral and popular vote landslide, it meant nothing to the South. To them the Northerner president Lincoln was but a stooge of the Yankees. None of the legislative debates bore any fruit and further discussion and debate just seemed to make things worse. By 1860, the writing was on the wall. Friends said goodbye to each other and Southerners living in the North reluctantly marched back home. West Point friends and comrades saying goodbye were especially poignant. There was the possibility that they would have to face each other in battle, and even most probably would be compelled to kill each other.

In 1860, the tremors leading to a huge national upheaval began. South Carolina, Mississippi, Florida, Alabama, Georgia, Louisiana, Texas, and Virginia seceded from the United States and created a new "country" called the Confederated States of America. These Confederates were now arrayed against their citizen fellowmen in the North, the Union.

When the first shots were fired in Fort Sumter in April of 1861, it showed that no amount of politics would salvage this gulf between morality and economics. Slavery was of course, just one reason why Americans were now fighting each other. States' rights, apportionment of new territories, and interstate commerce have been mentioned over the years as to the causes of the Civil War but the underlying theme was that the South needed slavery to continue and the North wanted them to relinquish it. Virgin, Arkansas, Tennessee and North Carolina would soon join the Confederated States of America. Politics had failed the country.

Over 200,000 combatants would die on the battlefield over the next four years as Americans fought each other bitterly. In addition up to 800.000 other combatants and civilians would die from wounds, disease, and starvation. This represented over 3 percent of the population of the country then. If such a war were waged today, it would mean that around 10 million Americans would die from the confrontation.

After four bitter years, the Union finally succeeded in overcoming the Confederates and slavery was going to be eradicated in North America. The politics was not as poisonous when the U.S. Congress debated but officially outlawed slavery through the passage of by 13th amendment to the U.S Constitution. The 14th amendment removed any barriers that blacks had towards citizenship as it defined what was correct due process and required due process regardless of race. Finally, the 15th Amendment accorded the right to vote for black men, rounding out the emancipation of black Americans.

<u>Rebuilding</u>

The politics in the years after the end of the civil war was all about managing the rapid expansion in population, territory, and commerce. The country's first transcontinental railroad was built and this stimulated a huge boom in economic activity and population movement. Alexander Graham Bell invented the telephone which led to a new era in communications. The politicians in U.S. Congress expanded the reach of government by creating the Department of Justice to help curtail increases in crime in the growing country, especially in the West.

Nine states were added in the 35 years between the end of the Civil War and the turn of the century, together with a slew of new federal government, agencies, and laws that seemed to increase the centralized powers in Washington D.C. In the 20th century, the U.S. would experience even more growth and see more innovations. Thomas Edison, Henry Ford, and the Wright brothers would catapult the country to never achieved before heights in technology, transportation, and innovation. The last couple of decades of 19th century U.S. is often referred to as the "Gilded Age," with a never-before seen accumulation of individual wealth and assets in American history.

It was a country that seemed to grow out of its britches every few years. The Founding Fathers would not have envisioned that their little band of about 2 million colonists in 13 states would explode to over forty states and 75 million people in 125 years. The country also tripled in land-size with the attendant flow of large groups of people to these new territories. The looming question was with the nation's increasing size and complexity, could the United States still afford to allow the least amount of governance from Washington, D.C.? Was it enough for the individual states to govern themselves? The states had big differences in size, population, and resources and there was a huge concern that some intervention was needed to smooth things out. Politics was about to play a big role as the nineteenth century was coming to a close.

By the end of the century it was becoming apparent that it was normal for a free-market economy that was the United States would suffer rises and dips in its economic fortunes. Every few years or so recessions would occur without any fixed lengths or intensity only to have the economy roar back again with a vengeance. These rises and dips in the "business cycles" would be used as political instruments (and sometimes clubs) for a political party to point out the failures of the other party and to extol the virtues of their own movement. But one thing was certain then as it is today: After a dip in economic activity, recession, or depression, the country comes roaring back at levels that exceeded any previous apex. It is the nature of American creativity, ingenuity, and persistence – large leaps of technology and business activity would lead to dramatic increases in economic activity but also precipitated sometimes scary declines.

After forty years being generally politics-free after the Civil War, the country was about to enter a new state of affairs as politics, economics, and ideology would soon coalesce.

<u>The "leftward" turn of America</u>

When many historians think of the deviation of the country from its "founding principles," the name of Woodrow Wilson surfaces prominently. He was an academician, a former president of Princeton University, who pored over minute details and considered every angle of and issue sometimes probably to the point of overthinking things. However, he was also a skillful politician who deftly overcame a comeback bid by the popular Theodore Roosevelt in the 1912 presidential elections. The Democrat Wilson beat Roosevelt and two other candidates in the electoral college 435-96 and won 40% of the popular vote beating Roosevelt by 2 million votes. William Howard Taft, the incumbent Republican, garnered 8 electoral votes and had less votes than Roosevelt who was essentially a third-party candidate.

In his campaign, Wilson sometimes sounded like fellow "modern" Democrats Barack Obama, Hillary Clinton, and Bernie Sanders at the height of their own campaign efforts. Wilson argued that property must take a backseat to humanity and espoused the principles advocated by his economic adviser, the attorney Louis D. Brandeis, who said that the government should play a big role in overseeing private corporate trusts.

The most interesting aspect of Woodrow Wilson's profile was his affection for the British constitutional system. If he wasn't an American citizen, he would have been very comfortable in British government which fascinated him. Unlike the United States constitution which was a fixed set of rules, Wilson was enamored by the British style were laws were evolving and changing and based on evolving events instead of being rooted in the past. This is the same approach that modern day Democrats favor when they choose judicial appointees especially to the Supreme Court. Emulating Wilson, they view the U.S. Constitution as a "living, breathing document" that should be changed as circumstances change.

He also debunked the separation of powers doctrine that he considered both irresponsible and inefficient. Wilson was a firm believer in more government intervention than less. He believed that government could be used as an instrument for settling national problems and ills. He observed that the separation of powers doctrine left government branches and agencies squabbling with one another creating inefficiencies, gridlock. Wilson believed that because of this friction within the government, public policy and initiatives would be difficult to implement. It blunted responsiveness and trust, two must-haves in government.

Wilson quickly proved that he was not just an agent for leftward change in words but in deed as well. Among the very first things he signed into law was an act establishing a national income tax eventually leading to the Internal Revenue Service (created in 1862) as the central tax collector on a nationalized level. This would have been anathema to the Founding Fathers who were staunchly against anything that smelled of a king collecting duties from his subjects. Wilson also established the Federal Reserve to centralize monetary policy, and the Federal Trade Commission to bring the federal government into the business of overseeing business which would have made the Founding Fathers, who wanted states' rights to be preserved as much as possible, recoil. Politics was now a club used by Wilson to chip away at the Founding Fathers' vision of unfettered commerce.

Wilson them appointed the left-leaning Brandeis to the Supreme Court to sway the Court to his more interventionist vision of government. Brandeis quickly established a reputation of being anti-Big Business, anti-consumerism, and pro-regulation. He was fulfilling judicially, the policy goals that the Executive branch in the person of Wilson, were advocating.

Wilson had launched the country into a new political sphere, the so-called "Progressive Era."

World War I arrived but the U.S. joined the fray late. Wilson as much of the country did, not want to get involved in a European melee that was being waged thousands of miles from U.S. shores. But it afforded Democrats an opportunity to finance the war effort by allowing them to raise tax rates. From a zero percent rate on the top income bracket when Wilson took office, the top income bracket went up to 67%. The country fell into recession in 1919, reeling from lower economic activity and investment from the higher top tax rates. This was aggravated with 4 million returning troops from WW I and contributed leading to high unemployment rates.

Wilson left office after his second term ended in 1920, and the country was left to a new breed of politicians. After suffering a stroke, he was not nominated by the Democrats as their presidential candidate in 1920 fearing that a weak-looking candidate had no chance to win the elections. The Democrats fielded a lesser-known James Cox, the governor of Iowa. The country by this time was war-weary and had just experienced a deep recession. Cox was soundly beaten by Republican Warren Harding, who vowed to go in the opposite direction of his predecessor.

Harding made good on his political promises by lowering federal income tax rates across the board and promoting businesses, especially the goliaths like Andrew Mellon the banking magnate, and led initiatives for the government to help businesses instead of adding restrictions and regulations as Wilson's administration had done. Harding had an active two years before he was felled by a stroke in 1923. He was succeeded by an even more fierce *laissez faire* or free market advocate in Calvin Coolidge, who was Harding's vice-president. The country's political direction was once again turned on its head.

Together, Harding and Coolidge intervened in business affairs but in a significantly much more unobtrusive manner. Coolidge was a reluctant president, almost in the mold of George Washington. He privately intimated that government should be as inobtrusive as possible and sometimes felt that his presidency was totally unneeded. Despite being considered as a shoo-in for re-election, he dropped out of the Republican primaries and ceded the presidency to Herbert Hoover, who demolished Democrat Al Smith in the popular vote and the electoral vote in 1928. Politically, Hoover's win was a rousing approval of Coolidge's and Harding's administration and many considered it as Coolidge's third term even while the blustery Hoover privately detested the quiet and unassuming Coolidge. Americans wanted to see more under Hoover, much, much more.

The country's Gross Domestic Product fell by almost 20% as a result of WW II and a recession under Wilson. When Coolidge left office, GDP had shot up by a 33% to an all-time high. Americans went on a buying frenzy as the economy zoomed again with new fortunes made by oil, transportation, and retail tycoons. During Harding's term, women were also finally given the right to vote, significantly increasing women's voices not only in the ballot box, but the right seemed to empower women to participate more in economic and market issues.

Hoover's first year in office saw economic activity reach even greater heights. In 1930, GDP breached $100 billion for the first time in history, and a record number of companies filed for incorporation and an increasing number of investors and businessmen wanted to participate in the heady economic times. Then things went horribly south.

<u>Depressing times</u>

There are an endless number of explanations as to what led to the 1929 Great Depression. It can be very easy to blame it on Big Business greed and the lack of adequate government intervention. There is a lot of anecdotal and statistical evidence to those factors, but there were many underlying reasons that contributed to the economic collapse. First, the economic results of other countries were all falling below expectations. This affected U.S. exports and was further worsened by Hoover passing the Smoot-Hawley tariff act that imposed many restrictions on foreign trade that may have worsened the Depression. Despite him being behind the tariff act, Hoover blamed the Great Depression on foreign factors instead of domestic issues. Second, the Federal Reserve created under Wilson eased U.S. monetary policy effectively "printing currency" which provided easily accessible financing to investors. Third but certainly not least, was the so-called orgy of speculation that investors engaged in right before the crisis. Corporations began to sell shares of stock of their companies over and above the true market value and their underlying assets. Investors couldn't have enough of stocks and the buying frenzy bloated stock prices to unrealistic levels. Hoover tried to duck this politically also when he referred to a statement that Coolidge made about stocks being undervalued.

When companies started to fail, investors discovered that they were holding on to paper that was just worth pennies. Billions of dollars of wealth disappeared and the economy took a severe nose-dive. By the end of Hoover's first term, the country's GDP was halved and his political future was doomed. Democrat Franklin Delano Roosevelt or FDR, drubbed Hoover in the 1932 elections winning 472 electoral votes to Hoover's 59, Roosevelt also carried 42 out of 48 states and won the popular vote with a margin of over 7 million votes. Roosevelt's victory ended an 12-year Republican era of unbridled capitalism and put himself firmly in place to continue Wilson's big government prescription to solve national ills.

<u>The New Deal was a Big Deal</u>

Roosevelt the former governor of New York had a plan to turn the country around. If allowing business and especially Big Business to roam unfettered had led to the Great Depression, then following the opposite tack seemed to make the most sense. He created dozens of government agencies to allow the government to micromanage specific aspects of American industry. They were the "Alphabet Soup" agencies that were identified by their three-letter acronyms. Seven of them still exist and exert significant power and influence over day to day corporate and private activity in the United States. These are:

Farm Credit Administration (FCA) - Make and oversee loans to farmers,

Federal Communications Commission (FCC) - Overseeing communications and electronic transmissions,

Federal Deposit Insurance Corporation (FDIC) - Provide free insurance to depositors,

Federal Housing Administration (FHA) - Oversee housing loans,

Securities and Exchange Commission (SEC) - Oversee corporations and monitor unusual activity,

Social Security Board (SSB), now the Social Security Administration - handling Americans' retirement funds, and

Tennessee Valley Authority (TVA) - Oversee energy and water resources in the Tennessee Valley.

From a political standpoint, Roosevelt tilted to the country to a "light" form of socialism - the political system where the government controls the factors of production while possessing punitive powers for those failing to adhere to his agencies' myriad rules and regulations.

Roosevelt like Wilson, appeared to have a disdain for the Separation of Powers doctrine that the Founding Fathers based their government on. The Supreme Court found that many of his agencies were trampling on individual and states' constitutional rights and blocked some of his executive decrees. Frustrated by his ability to secure favorable judgements regarding his agencies, he proposed to add additional justices to Supreme Court to increase the number of justices from nine to fifteen. Being the sitting president with a decisive edge in numbers in the Senate, he could ensure that at least six (the new ones he would have appointed) of fifteen votes would tilt his way. This "court-packing" was packaged as the Judicial Procedures Reform Bill of 1937. But the U.S. Senate decisively voted down the measure by fifty votes, allowing their conscience to side with the Founding Fathers rather than the seemingly power-hungry FDR.

The turn to the left politically was met with a lot of fanfare. The FDR administration seemed to pattern some of the unveilings of the new agencies after openings of groceries and Broadway shows. Absent were the banners, ribbon-cuttings, and celebrity sightings but the 3-letter acronyms stood out. All the big government activity earned FDR an even more resounding reelection victory in 1936. Massive government spending increased the GDP by 40% since he took office. He trounced Republican Alf Landon by winning 523 electoral votes versus 8 for Landon. FDR also carried 46 out of 48 states and beat Landon by over 11 million votes, an unprecedented margin.

FDR's second term however, quickly ran into trouble. There seemed to be a limit to what government expenditure could do for an economy. The economy began to contract and suffered a recession that lasted for a year beginning in the last quarter of 1937, just months after FDR's inauguration before his presidency was apparently rescued by an unlikely European tyrant.

<u>The War economy and post-war United States</u>

Adolf Hitler, the previously unremarkable Viennese soldier was draping the world with his fascist and racist visions of a New World Order that was run by blue-eyed Aryans and those willing to capitulate to, and serve him. Hitler's Germany began occupying European countries in 1938 with its annexation of Czechoslovakia and Austria. Hitler and Germany were on a country-stealing rampage what its disciplined military and the size and strength of its men and materiel.

For FDR it seemed like World War I all over again. He bitterly remembered the millions of men that the U.S. sent to Europe with 116,000 never coming back alive. He also remembered the deep recession and unemployment that befell the country after the war ended, creating a huge blemish on Woodrow Wilson's record. While the pace of Germany's conquests was swift and troubling, FDR did not want to commit resources of his country's flailing economy to a remote war that did not directly impact the U.S. That is until Germany's Axis partner Japan, attacked Pearl Harbor in Hawaii on December 7, 1941.

World War II provided FDR two invaluable gifts that a politician could only dream about. First, it allowed him to look presidential. He was already wheelchair-bound after being afflicted by polio, but his speechwriters were adept in writing soaring elegies about crises, national unity, and persistence in the face of crisis. There was no better political cover for a president than to vow that he was going to save the country from evil oppressors, just as George W. Bush would do some sixty years later with the 9/11 attacks. His "Day of Infamy" speech declaring the country's entry into World War II masked the increasing concerns about the economy which was barely recovering from its last recession.

But more than looking presidential, it allowed the Executive office to appropriate resources to the war machinery, and further increase the grip of the Federal government. Steel, rubber, and textiles were swallowed in this machinery to manufacture the guns, equipment, uniforms, and armaments that the U.S. would soon put to bear. The war effort temporarily gave people jobs and when the soldiers returned from the end of WWII the country experienced a short recession. The country overcame the low end of the business cycle rather quickly after the recession, but the U.S. had to move on without FDR who would have been a shoo-in to win an unheard of fourth term in office. He died in 1945 while posing for a portrait.

<u>A post-war boom that never came</u>

Harry S. Truman, the unassuming haberdasher from Missouri, like Calvin Coolidge did not seek the presidency. He had to make probably the most consequential decision in military history then and since: dropping the atomic bombs in Japan to end the war and establishing the United States as the world's pre-eminent "superpower." There was very little politics in Truman's first term as the nation sat back and waited how an inexperienced unelected president would perform in rebuilding a nation after a much revered and active FDR. Politically, he was viewed not only as the person in charge of rebuilding America but the entire world, including former enemies Germany and Japan. The U.S. economy was trying to come back slowly but the country was still in shambles and GDP fell by just under ten percent from the end of the war. The presidential elections were looming and the Republicans were seeing an excellent opportunity to wrest the presidency after sixteen years of Democratic rule.

The Republicans selected Thomas Dewey for the 1948 elections and the New York native and ex-governor seemed to have the charisma, experience, and big state support needed to win. He also had history behind him. FDR and Theodore Roosevelt were former New York governors who had easily won first terms as president. Dewey ran like an incumbent confident that the pre-election polls that gave him comfortable leads would hold. He spoke in generalities and relied on the general unlikability of Truman and the sluggish economy that was dragging behind him. In what was the start of a partisan shift, Truman targeted consumers, farmers, labor and black Americans. From the beginning of its inception the Republican party had always been seen as the party of the black man, with the Civil War a stark example of the party's commitment to minorities. In a close election with so much at stake Truman went for the black vote as Dewey, the elite white man from New York, campaigned like a Caucasian Rotary Club president.

On election day in 1948 it seemed that Dewey had the race in the bag, fighting Truman neck and neck as the results from the Eastern states came in. The pro-Republican Chicago Daily Tribune had published an early edition announcing in a headline that Dewey had won. In reality, Truman took an early small lead in the voting and never relinquished it. In the closest vote in the 20th century to date, Truman edged Dewey by just 1.2 million votes winning razor thin victories in California, Illinois, and Ohio. With eleven million votes and 78 electoral college votes, Truman won those three states by a COMBINED 58 THOUSAND votes. If Dewey had flipped those states, he would have won the presidency instead.

<u>A new threat</u>

Truman, who became the only man to drop the atomic bomb in wartime was now forced to turn his attention from national politics to geo-politics. The U.S. discovered that Russia through American spies had been stealing atomic bomb plans, a suspicion that was confirmed when Russian detonated its first test bomb in 1949. Truman had already pursued a program of Russian containment before his re-election win and he not trust Russian president Joseph Stalin and communism. Truman's Russian containment policy became known as the Truman Doctrine, a political coup that added heft to his name in the pantheon of presidents.

Americans in general, and not only Truman became suspicious of Russians and the dual ideologies that they represented: Communism and socialism. The two political doctrines in most Americans' minds were anathema to the American culture of rugged individualism and personal freedom. Most of the U.S. Constitution and the Declaration of Independence essentially codified these sentiments and there was no room for compromising with Russian ideologies.

Communism assures that everyone is equal and no one is poor or wealthy. The communist system dictates that the working class as a group owns everything with very limited personal possessions. The small but powerful group leaders in a communist system controls all the factors of production and distributes the fruits of production based on what the leaders think the working class needs; usually little more than minimum. There are few luxuries or amenities that communist working-class people own as opposed to the conspicuous consumption enjoyed and displayed by Americans.

It was these systems, especially communism that spooked America. While communists had organized themselves in the 20's and 30's, they were considered as fringe group irritants and elicited very little attention. When Russia detonated their nuclear bomb and their imperialist motives were unmasked, communists became Enemy Number 1 in the United States.

A "Red Scare" ensued with politicians like the Republican Joseph McCarthy led investigations of people or groups that they considered as sympathetic to the communist cause. The most prominent of these investigations was the probe of Hollywood figures leading to the "blacklisting" of many workers including prominent actors and directors.

When Russia threatened to take over the Korean peninsula in 1950, a proxy war began as the U.S. sent forces to defend the Korean peninsula. After a tense standoff, the war "ended" in 1953 with Korean being split into northern and southern halves. While the U.S. and Russia did not directly face each other in the battlefield, a silent but potentially deadly tension developed between the two countries – the Cold War.

The U.S. would now be in a permanent geopolitical state of tension with its enemies. Truman had ushered in a new model of governance for all future presidents – they not only had to manage the country's internal situation, they also had to deal with how the world reacted to, and treated the world's superpower.

It was going to be tough going for the coming presidents Republican or Democrat. The Republicans finally broke through in 1952 when Dwight Eisenhower, a popular WW II general won the presidency easily in that year's elections, the first Republican in the White house in twenty years. Eisenhower the military veteran seemed to be just what the country needed with simmering international tensions. Russia and China began to take over countries in the Indo-China region which led Eisenhower to propound his "Domino Theory" where he believed that the Indo-Chinese countries would "fall like dominoes" until every country in the region was under communist control.

This fear led the United Sates to getting embroiled in the Vietnam War, with Eisenhower's Democrat successor John F. Kennedy ordering U.S. troops into another battle far from the country's shores. After Kennedy's assassination in 1963, Lyndon B. Johnson reluctantly continued to get the U.S. involved even if his heart and priority was to "fix" domestic issues like poverty and racial equality. Misleading information from the generals in the field and the surprising resilience of the enemy North Vietnamese forces appeared to suck the U.S. into an "unwinnable" situation, leading Johnson to eventually step down from the presidency instead of running for reelection in 1968. Politics and geo-politics conspired to make him quit his job as the most powerful man in the world, because in the end he could not harness that power to defeat the U.S. enemies.

The Vietnam War and the ensuing protests and agitation against it signaled a new era in U.S. politics. In every election up to Lyndon Johnson, the country selected its president because it was voting with its pocketbook and the safety of its country. The country would soon be divided along the lines of ideology instead of survival and self-defense.

Chapter Four: Modern Day Politics

Entering the 1960's the country emerged as the world's premiere military superpower where it earned its reputation as the liberator of helpless and downtrodden masses of people. But this abundance of wealth and power set in motion a new era of collective self-reflection as the mighty United States, fattened by economic affluence and military superiority became the perfect breeding ground for dissension and doubt. For the first time, Americans allowed themselves to scrutinize and criticize the merits and more significantly, the downside of its successes.

A "New Awakening" was dawning on a well-fed nation in a growing culture of collective introspection and questioning. The United States possessed the resources and the willingness to help former enemies rise up from the ashes with arrangements like the Marshall Plan which allotted (in current prices) over one trillion dollars in aid to European countries including its former enemies. If it liberated countries and entire continents why did it continue to have helpless and downtrodden masses within its own borders? If it could afford to amass immense wealth and spend it on weapons to liberate countries, why couldn't it use some of those resources to liberate its own people from the depths of poverty? Why was there segregation and huge differences in the standard of living between different races? And finally did the country really need a huge military apparatus given the overwhelming successes and the defeat of its major enemies?

In the wake of this national self-reflection the seeds of dissent were being gradually sown. It was cultivated by a combination of radical activists and college intellectuals whose message of railing against the "establishment" began to resonate in a country bored by peace and wracked by guilt. In the early 60's, agitating for racial and Civil Rights was a fashionable precursor to a greater revolution. Certainly, there were legitimate issues especially on the subject of race. There was no room in any compassionate and noble Republic for segregated bathrooms, buses and drinking fountains. The era's mood was the perfect spawning ground for opportunists to seize the legitimate issues as the takeoff point for fame, recognition and wealth. The players in the emerging modern liberal movement were quickly realizing that the country could afford to foot the bill for some internal agitation. This mood of disquiet was the perfect setting from which the antiwar and American-style socialist movements was born. A new political class, the liberals were emerging and a new debate on rights was about to begin.

The Civil Rights Movement of the 1960's firmly established an American progressive arm that today supports the Democratic Party and its political network. The anti-war movement, the support for racial equality, and the expansion of the federal government are the linchpins of the movement - The era of modern U.S. politics started in the sixties.

Before Lyndon Johnson resigned from the presidency, he managed to turn the country even more leftward as if he was continuing unfinished work by FDR. He declared a "War on Poverty" as part of his "Great Society" vision. He created Medicare and Medicaid which instantly health insurance coverage for a large swathe of the country, especially the elderly. The Department of Housing and Urban Development (HUD) was also established to help socialize housing with the goal of providing a home for everyone who needed one. He also signed the first federal gun control law in the history of the country, defying the Second Amendment and alienating gun owners.

The biggest initiative of Johnson's presidency however, was the passing of the Civil Rights Act which immediately shifted allegiances of blacks from Republican to Democrat. The "War on Poverty" also allowed the Democrats to proclaim that they were the party of the poor and the underprivileged. The Civil Rights Act did not only address the rights of blacks, but also women as well, and it seemed that the Democrats had cornered a huge voting bloc to their side.

The Civil Rights movement was coinciding with the increased agitation by black leaders against the rampant discrimination against them. While Martin Luther King Jr., Rosa Parks and other brave figures fought for equality in racial treatment, it was only in the 1960's that the country and world noticed their growing unrest and dissatisfaction. By the time the 1968 elections came about, the country was well on its way to establishing political sides – who belonged to the right and left and why.

The Vietnam War created a militant leftist movement that not only protested the U.S. involvement in Vietnam, but a whole slew of demands designed to cast doubt and suspicion about the "Establishment" comprised of the rich, big business, and the military. The movement was made up of mostly of entitled Caucasian college students and militant black activists who needed all the exposure that they could get. This protest movement was unfortunately infiltrated by committed Communists and Russian interlocutors whose goal was to cause disruption and create a rift in American society. Public protests especially in campuses increased and conflated with the anti-war sentiment, the protest movements won a lot of followers, adherents, and admirers.

Liberal vs. Conservative

In the United States, left and right issues transformed into what was liberal and what was conservative. In general, if someone wanted to stick to the original intent of the Constitution and preserve as much as much personal liberty and states' rights, it would be considered a conservative stance. If someone is an advocate of a "living" U.S. Constitution that changed with the times as Woodrow Wilson saw it, this would be considered a liberal view. From a governance point of view, more government intervention was a liberal view and less government intrusion would be conservative. This was reversed on the personal liberty side: less intrusion into personal activities was a liberal view and a more restrictive approach on personal freedoms was conservative. For liberals this meant mostly that they should be able to do anything they want short of murder and stealing.

From a foreign affairs standpoint even with resolve shown by FDR and Truman during WWII and the Korean War, the anti-war protests in the 1960's won the attention and affection of a large part of American society. The war correspondents covering the Vietnam War seemed to be in an adversarial relationship with the American generals directing the war. In the growing age of television, the media reported the lies and distortions that the U.S. command in Vietnam on daily basis. The public not only began to see the Vietnam War as a waste of resources and American lives, but many began to view the military as an oppressive, ruthless, and corrupt tool of politicians and Big Business.

But politics was more that theory in the 20th century. As we saw in Chapter 3 Wilson and FDR departed from the Founding Fathers' aversion to big government and created laws and agencies to increase the reach and influence of the federal government. Conversely, Harding and Coolidge were pretty much hands-off on the economic side of things. When Eisenhower won the presidency he became associated with the military and U.S. offensive strategy. Being a Republican, support for the military became synonymous with supporting Republicans. Even if John F. Kennedy and Lyndon B. Johnson were responsible for sending troops to Vietnam and escalating U.S. involvement, the horrors of warfare and military excesses were attributed to the Republican supported military and then to Johnson successor Richard Nixon who was the sitting president when the war was winding down. Nixon's successor Gerald Ford was in the White House when the United States shamefully "lost" its first war. Instead of lamenting the U.S. withdrawal, many cheered the embarrassing defeat of the U.S. In less than a generation, American soldiers were now hated having been revered as heroes when they fought in WWII.

<u>Republican and Democrats align with the issues</u>

Let us look at how the two major political parties evolve to their current editions.

With the left and right sides in politics having been drawn to opposing sides in the debate government and the military, a major political upheaval ensued arising out of the Civil Rights movement in the 60's – the redefining of "rights."

<u>Victims and the evolving concept of "rights"</u>

The U.S. Constitution includes a Bill of Rights that lays out a laundry list of rights that accrue to citizens and states. These were laid out in the first ten amendments to the U.S. Constitution and included the following individual rights:

1. Freedom of speech;

2. Freedom of (and freedom from a national) religion;

3. The right to peacefully assemble;

4. Freedom of the press;

5. The right to bear arms;

6. Freedom from unwarranted arrests, seizures, and searches;

7. Freedom from self-incrimination;

8. Right to speedy trial and trial by jury of peers;

In addition, the U.S. Constitution suggested sweeping powers to the states, according them all powers that the constitution did not give to the federal government. To further show that the

Founding Fathers wanted the states to have more power, the Tenth amendment states that the federal government will only have those powers that the U.S. Constitution grants it.

The Civil Rights movement quickly led to the expansion of what rights Americans had. For liberals this was a major development because the creation of new rights could now be left to any branch of government without necessarily amending the Constitution which required significant majority approval from the U.S. legislature: Two-thirds majority votes in both the U.S. Senate and the U.S. House of Representatives.

The Civil Rights Act gave blacks and minorities federal protection and ensured the black citizens possessed the same rights as other races in access to public locations and made it a federal crime to discriminate against applicants and employees on the basis of sex, religion, national origin, and more importantly in the context of the 60's rights movement, race. It has since been expanded by the liberal movement to included illegal aliens (now called undocumented immigrants) and the lesbian, gay, bisexual, and transgender (LGBT) "community."

The momentum of the rights movement began to push "conservatives" into a corner. The tidal wave of what they felt were affronts to the constitution were coming in hard, fast, and unstoppable. The Civil Rights tsunami broke the dam, and conservatives are still tilting at the windmills until today to fend it off.

The debate about rights is at the forefront of what it is to be liberal and conservative today.

Chapter Five: Liberal vs. Conservative?

Chapter 4 discussed how United States politics was bifurcated into liberal and conservative factions. The notion of government reach, foreign intervention, religion, and especially "rights" are the issues that are hotly debated and fought about today from bar rooms and dinner tables all the way to the Capitol and the White House. It is useful to identify the major issues about which liberals and conservatives wage bitter battles.

<u>SOCIAL ISSUES</u>

<u>Abortion</u>

The "right" to abortion was one that was bitterly fought in the 60's until the U.S. Supreme Court in 1973 criminalized the restriction to access to abortion. This is one of the most inflammatory issues in politics today. Liberals and conservatives still play a game of tug of war with the strengthening and weakening of state and federal abortion laws. Abortion is the litmus test in confirmation hearings for confirming justices of the Supreme Court. The right to and choosing to have an abortion has morphed to someone being "pro-choice" and preserving "reproductive rights."

Liberals: They argue that a women should have domain over her body and that only she can determine what happens to her body including whether she wants a have a baby issue forth from her body. They feel that protecting a woman's choice as to whether she wants to carry a baby to term is one of the most important female rights that helps women restrict male dominance and control.

Conservatives: They call themselves "pro-life." Conservatives contend that the issue is simply a case of being pro-abortion and anti-abortion and that any other description is merely skirting the issue. They bristle at the pro-choice label that pro-abortion advocates use asking why the two other parties to a pregnancy, the male and the unborn fetus/baby seemed to have been forgotten in the choice angle of the issue. They also invoke the morality of extinguishing a human life arbitrarily and not giving the male responsible for the new life any voice in the matter. The abortion issue also led to the definition of "fetus" as arguments have raged whether one, the new life is simply a mass of tissue and cells called a fetus, or a human being, and two at what point is the fetus or baby considered human. This has further led to defining at which trimester a baby in the woman's womb is capable of life outside the mother's womb.

<u>Climate change</u>

Liberals: Humans are the main cause of climate change, and regulations should be put in place to help mitigate climate change. According to liberals, man-made global or "anthropogenic" warming (MMGW) is the biggest threat to humanity's existence. Former Vice-President Al Gore Jr.'s Oscar winning documentary on the dangers of global warming, *An Inconvenient Truth,* followed his own *Earth in the Balance,* a best-selling book which details the deleterious effects of the internal combustion engine that has powered automobiles for the past century. Gore Jr. a non-scientist, argues that MMGW is the source of most natural disasters and natural disasters in the making. If one googles the term "global warming" and pair it with any type of natural calamity. There are many alluding to a "scientific report" that links MMGW to many of Mother Nature's mishaps. MMGW is pointed out as the cause of a multitude of natural calamities and disasters: hurricanes, tornadoes, glaciers shrinking, huge wildfires burning swathes of pristine forest; oceans' water levels rising; increases and decreases in certain animal population; drought periods because of too little rain; and flooding in certain areas because of too much rain. The George Soros liberal think tank the *Center for American Progress* listed the top 100 effects of global warming, ranging from the loss of French wines to baby penguins. They hammer home the fact that 97% of scientists agree that there is climate change which proves beyond reasonable doubt that climate change is caused by man.

Conservatives: They maintain that climate change has been happening since the ice age, and humans have very little effect on climate so no regulations are required. Conservatives also counter that the world has warmed by just over 1 percent since they began "measuring" world wide temperature the past 150 years. They also believe that climate change is a new acronym that liberals created when the world stopped warming and now use any change in climate as an excuse to create regulations to control human behavior. Finally, they ask (1) What is the ideal target temperature that the world needs (2) What measures need to be taken if world temperature drops or rises outside this ideal target temperature and (3) Who manages and monitors these measures?

Environment

Liberals: They believe that because mankind continues to mess up the environment, strict regulations are needed to prevent the environment from getting even more messed up. They also contend that the environment is increasingly getting poisoned, polluted, and contaminated by human activity. Stricter laws and regulations are needed to help contain the rampant abuse on mother nature.

Conservatives: Humans can be relied up to be responsible with the environment and progress ensures that responsible citizens will clean up after them. They also point out that the more advanced countries like the United States are "responsible" in their treatment of the environment because they know that a clean environment results in more efficient economies and systems. Additional does is adds significant costs to do business and reduce incentives for businesses to expand and innovate.

Foreign involvement in wars

Liberals: They say that the U.S. has no business in fighting the wars of other countries and the country should not waste American lives, money, and resources thousands of miles away when no U.S. interests are being compromised, or any U.S. lives are being endangered. Money is better spent on local programs.

Conservatives: The U.S. has an important role keeping peace in the world and it is in its best interest to keep tyrants in check. They also emphasize the importance of showing muscle and force abroad because the U.S. should protect its "friends" and keep tyrants from spreading their influence around the globe. It is more efficient to prevent terrorists and U.S. enemies from hatching plans to create problems rather than having to fight them when they have gathered enough strength and have become more lethal enemies.

<u>Gay rights including gay marriage</u>

Liberals: The LGBT community should be afforded the same rights as any other citizen in the U.S. Recent "victories" such as gay marriage and a third bathroom for the transgendered are big steps but more should be done to battle discrimination against them.

Conservatives: The LGBT community already enjoys many rights but there should be some restrictions on their lifestyle because these contravene religious values on which the U.S. was founded.

<u>Gun control</u>

Liberals: They assert that guns should be controlled even more and the Second Amendment of the U.S. Constitution should be either significantly amended or even repealed. They also point out the horrendous shootings in schools to help prove that current gun laws do not protect ordinary citizens from gun owners. There is no room for automatic weapons and other more lethal armaments in a modern society. Many liberals are asking for a serious look into whether the Second Amendment of the U.S. Constitution should be repealed or significantly altered

Conservatives: Guns are a constitutional right and should be as less curtailed as possible. They also argue that the deaths from the highly publicized shootings are more than balanced out by the lives saved when ordinary citizens are able to protect themselves from undesirable elements.

<u>Health care</u>

Liberal – Everyone should be entitled to healthcare, free or paid for. They point out that "progressive" countries like Canada and the United Kingdom provides at least basic healthcare everyone. It is unconscionable that an affluent and advanced country like the U.S. cannot have some sort of universal or single-payer healthcare system to provide healthcare to everyone.

Conservative – The United States cannot afford to cover just anyone for free. They argue that with Medicare, Medicaid, and private and government employee programs, a big majority of Americans are already covered by insurance. The U.S. has the best and most innovative health care and drug industries in the world accounting for most of the world's innovations and breakthroughs. Forcing doctors and hospitals to accept less money for the sake of cheap and affordable coverage would drive them out of the industry and allow health care quality to slip. Many Canadians go to the U.S. whenever they need doctors with specialized skills.

Immigration

Liberal – Illegal aliens in the country should be given a chance for citizenship especially for their children born in the United States. They believe that the U.S. should be more "welcoming" to those who end up in the country illegally. They liken the "undocumented immigrants" to the Europeans coming to Ellis Island beginning in the late 18th century. The country should remember the U.S.'S traditional principle of being warm hosts for the "huddled masses" that are simply fleeing their world of repression and poverty.

Conservative – Illegal aliens should be treated as criminals just like everyone who has broken the law. They are appalled that illegal aliens are even recognized as immigrants because they have clearly violated U.S. law and sovereignty. They point out that most countries strictly enforce immigration laws and have a much stricter approach with illegal aliens than the U.S. They also point out that illegal aliens especially those coming across the border form Mexico bring in a lot of illegal drugs and could be a potential source of terrorist activity.

Military and police

Liberals - Military and police should be reined in because they can be abusive with their power. They point out that point out that police have a dismal reputation especially in minority communities because of racial profiling and brutality. Ever since the Rodney King a black man was beaten up by white police officers in Los Angeles in 1991, liberals point out many cases of racial profiling that have led to injuries and deaths of many racial minorities in the hands of police. They also criticize many military commanders for their sometime dim view of the battle-readiness of women and gays in the military.

Conservatives – Military and police should be given as much support as they can and that they should be given the benefit of the doubt because they put their lives on the line daily. They argue that police perform a very dangerous job and that they have an overwhelmingly good record in protecting citizens despite isolated cases of abuse.

Minority rights

Liberals - Minorities have been abused in the past so they should be extended at least equal the amount of rights that Caucasians are entitled to. Despite the Civil Rights Act, affirmative action, and the Equal Employment Opportunity laws there is still a long way to go before minorities and especially black people can be considered equal to their Caucasian countrymen.

Conservatives - Minorities already have the same rights as Caucasians and their rights should not exceed those of other citizens. They stress that the Declaration of Independence decreed that all men are CREATED equal but not necessarily have to END UP being equal. Equal outcomes for everyone is the hallmark of communism and socialism.

Religion

Liberals – There should be as little displays of religion as possible to prevent people from feeling left out and to prevent tyranny from religious groups.

Conservatives – People should be allowed to practice and display their faith whenever they feel like it. They believe that school prayer should be returned to public schools to provide children a peaceful avenue for quiet, peaceful, and thoughtful introspection and prayer.

School choice

Liberals: Public schools do a good job at educating students through high schools so the current system of making kids go to school in their own district should be continued. The country's public school system needs all the support they can get, and this traditional backbone of U.S. education should be strengthened and not diluted by sucking off funds for voucher programs.

Conservatives: Parents should be allowed to choose what schools they should go to regardless of where they live and parents should be given the resources to do so. They maintain that the public school system through their teachers' unions help further the modern liberal agenda by indoctrinating children with liberal social issues in abortion and homosexuality. Conservatives also point out that in many public schools, the acquisition of basic skills is only secondary to the political programming of the youngest and most impressionable of our citizens. During these early stages, teachers' unions in the public school system make sure that the message and agenda of modern liberalism are dispensed with maximum impact and effect. In the recent George W. Bush and Donald Trump presidencies, many public school teachers at every level invoke Adolf Hitler and Nazism not in its historical context, but to suggest comparisons to Bush, Trump and other Republicans.

Welfare

Liberals – The U.S. is a rich enough and should offer welfare to as many people who need it. An extensive and easily accessible welfare system is an indication of an enlightened and compassionate government.

Conservatives – The welfare system has always been broken and needs fixing because even because even people who do not need can avail of benefits. The point out that the over 25 trillion dollars spent on racial minorities over the past 50 years have not helped most minorities boost themselves.

ECONOMIC ISSUES

Energy dependence

Liberals: They want to minimize and even stop the exploiting natural resources. They maintain that all the drilling for oil in its various forms are harming the environment. U.S. Democratic lawmakers have threatened to "socialize" oil production and distribution and eradicate the oil companies' "greed-motivated exploitation" of natural resources. Speaker of the House Nancy Pelosi in the past has furious at what she believed to be the source of the problem: the producers (especially foreign producers) themselves. She once even warned of possible lawsuits to be filed against the tight global coalition of oil producers, the Organization of Petroleum Exporting Countries or OPEC. Even the middlemen didn't not escape the public rebuke by Democrat lawmakers They threatened to somehow "control" speculation in the futures market - the buying and selling platform that plays a big role in determining the market price of crude oil.

Conservatives: They want the country to thoroughly explore suspected reserves the so that the U.S. can be energy dependent. Conservatives have acknowledged that in the past ten years or so higher crude oil prices have translated to record highs at the retail pump even at inflation-adjusted levels. But they argue that these price increases is a simpoe supply-and-demand phenomenon: Americans consume 25% of the world's oil, as it is world's largest market for V-8 powered automobiles, SUVs, luxury cars, boats and planes. The United States also has the most airlines, airplanes and with 50,000 miles of paved highways it has the largest highway system by far in the world. In addition, the energy requirements of the world's largest number of servers to serve the Googles, Facebooks, and Twitters add to the energy load. The U.S. should have more of a free rein on its own resources so that it can tap so much more undiscovered resources to ensure "energy security" for generations to come.

Minimum wage

Liberals – All employees should be given a "living wage" allowing them to live on their salaries. They argue that entry level and under-educated people are not given a fair shake when they have to work on wages that can barely sustain their living expenses.

Conservatives – The market should be the major factor that dictates how much employees get paid, and not government-mandated salaries that are often unrealistic. When wages are hiked arbitrarily through government fiat, the usual result are high prices and the need to reduce their workforce to compensate for the higher salary levels.

Regulation

Liberals – Regulation assures that businesses conform to good practices to keep them from mistreating and abusing the public.

Conservatives – Onerous regulations increase the cost of business, drive up prices, and blunt innovation. The cost of running the government also rises significantly because of the costs associated with the monitoring and enforcement required to make sure regulations are complied with.

<u>Taxes</u>

Liberals –"Rich" Americans and corporations should be taxed as high as high as possible while others' tax rates should be as low as possible and in many cases even eradicated. The very rich can afford to still live very comfortably off whatever "net" cash flow remains after paying off their taxes. They point out that in the 50's the tax rates on the rich were very high and they were still able to pay for extravagant lifestyles.

Conservatives – High taxes at any bracket whether individual or corporate causes the economy to slow down because it discourages investment and blunts innovation. They maintain that it promotes the concealment and squirreling away of investible funds that could be reinvested into the economy. They point out that tax cuts passed during the administrations of John F. Kennedy and Ronald Reagan helped jump start moribund economies that were coming from high-tax regimes.

<u>Tort Reform</u>

Liberals – Lawyers should be given a free reign in prosecuting cases especially against abusive large companies and industries. It is the right of every American to seek redress from abuses especially those from the powerful and rich.

Conservatives – They charge that litigation is out of control. People use lawsuits in place of civil resolution of personal conflicts. They believe that substantial tort reform should include instituting some form of a loser pays trial system similar to those in Europe to discourage the filing of frivolous lawsuits.

<u>Who are liberal and conservative?</u>

Conservatives' battle against liberals have become much harder because the liberals' cheering section has become all that much bigger and formidable. The following groups overwhelmingly support liberal issues over conservative issues:

1. The public school system – Represented by the giant National Education Association which is a public elementary and high school teacher's union of 3 million. Their voting bloc is solidly Democrat and they support most of the social issues that liberals espouse;

2. University professors – Recent surveys have disclosed that nine out of ten professors are either registered Democrats or have liberal leanings;

3. Newspapers and magazines – They are scorned by conservatives as the "mainstream media" and their reporting is decidedly pro-Democrat and liberal. Recent measurements show that over 90 percent of their reportage on Donald Trump has been negative while Obama negative media coverage never exceeded 25%. In presidential endorsements, the major newspapers favoring

Hillary Clinton over Trump in 2016 were about 90%, a trend that slightly exceeded Obama's 70% cumulative totals over Mitt Romney in 2012 and John McCain in 2008;

4. Television and Hollywood personalities and associated arts – Campaign contributions from Hollywood and other entertainment types run about 95% Democrat. In 2016 lucrative campaign fund-raisers were sponsored by among others; Beyonce, Justin Timberlake, and George Clooney.

5. Government workers – The American Federation of Government Employees consisting of over 670,000 mostly federal employees practically vote as a bloc for Democrat candidates;

6. Labor Unions – Large umbrella organizations such as the AFL-CIO have long supported liberal programs of government-mandated wages and benefits. They believe that conservatives and Republicans are the tool of "big business" and wealthy people;

6. Racial minorities – In the last six presidential elections in the U.S., at least 90% of African-Americans have voted for the Democratic candidate. They feel that Democrats support their agitation for equal rights and resist Republican's efforts to curtail social programs such as welfare;

7. Attorneys – They resist all suggestion of significant tort reform which Republicans and conservatives continue to suggest;

On the flipside, the following groups consistently throw their support behind conservative causes:

1. Fundamentalist Christians – The support mostly the social issues that conservatives agitate for especially religion;

2. Military and police – They appreciate conservatives' and Republican support for their jobs. Democrats have tended to slash military budgets and join in the efforts of anti-police activists; and

3. Small business owners – They are most affected by liberal government overreach on taxes and regulation.

Curiously a big schism has developed in "big business" support which is represented by large corporations. If political contributions are to be used as a gauge, the traditional industrial, energy and retail powerhouses contribute more to Republicans while the "new" money represented by billionaires in Wall Street and in "high-tech" where Sillion Valley billionaires and employees overwhelmingly support liberal causes and Democratic candidates. It used to be that demonizing rich people was the exclusive domain of liberals. They disparaged capitalism as a system that creates a deep wedge between the poorest and richest citizens who also own most of the country's wealth. They cannot attack capitalism and big business as much anymore because a big chunk of the money used in their activists efforts are funded by liberal- and Democrat-leaning billionaires. In *Forbes* magazine's list of the top 10 richest men in America for 2017, eight of the ten are heavy Democrat contributors.

.

Chapter Six: American Politics and the Rest of the World's

<u>The "better" Democrat</u>

When Barack Obama stepped down as U.S. President after eight years in office, IPSOS, an international marketing and research conducted a "worldwide poll" of 18,000 people under the age of sixty-five years old. The respondents came from the U.S. and Canada in North America; Turkey, Sweden, Spain, Poland, Italy, Hungary, Germany, the U.K., France, Belgium in Europe; South Korea, Japan, India, China, and Australia in Asia and Oceania; South Africa, Saudi Arabia, and Israel in African and the Middle East; and Peru, Mexico, and Argentina in South America.

The poll showed that almost 80% of respondents approved of Obama's presidency. The same poll, conducted just after Trump's inauguration showed that only about a third, 33% said that Trump would do a good job as president. These polls do not deviate that much from similar measurements made when the contrasted ex-presidents Bill Clinton, a Democrat and George W. Bush, a Republican. While the rest of the world by an 80-20 margin considers Democrats as better presidents, the United States remains firmly fifty-fifty in their own assessment as to whether a Democrat or Republican administration does a better job in governing.

The championing of American liberalism's ideals has extended beyond America's borders. The foreign media like the U.S. mainstream media, is overwhelmingly left leaning and much more critical of conservatives and Republicans than they are of modern liberals and Democrats. Magazines like The Economist and the Far Eastern Economic Review, together with almost every major newspaper outside of the United States exhaled collectively with the exit of George W. Bush and the descent of Barack Obama from the political heavens. Over two hundred thousand people listened to the first ever speech given by an American presidential candidate, Barack Obama on foreign soil. Poll after poll of foreigners and newspaper and magazine endorsements have displayed this one-sidedness in viewpoint regarding politics in the United States.

Even that supposed paragon of diplomacy and equality, the United Nations, parrots liberal politicians and operatives in the United States. The U.N. appears to share the foreign policy goals: Lots of rhetoric with nominal or no action. The U.N., like their liberal counterparts in the United States, seem to support totalitarians more than they do the U.S. For example, the organization appointed the late Ugandan despot Idi Amin to the United Nations Commission on Human Rights and its Security Council includes those bastions of communist repression, China and Russia. They have also watched with relative passivity while Africans enslave and murder each other while issuing love taps on the wrists to known state sponsors of terrorism. It does not help that Republican presidents have called for the U.N. to change their tune in supporting countries hostile to the U.S. Recent Republican presidents have held back membership payments to the U.N. once reaching $1.3 billion.

What accounts for the wide disparity in how Americans and the rest of the world view U.S politics?

<u>Media</u>

In Chapter Five, we saw how the media is overwhelmingly represented by liberals and generally left-leaning editors and reporters. The surge towards the left means that the reporting slant will also lean significantly leftward. A vast majority of people outside the United States are at best casual followers of American politics. They will get their U.S. political reporting in their countries through AP, Reuters, UPI, and CNN for the most part. If 80% if reporting in the political ether is left-leaning then 80% of what they read will be left leaning. After all, if CNN, The New York Times, AP, and UPI agree on the same take on a particular issue, then they must accurate.

The most influential European news reporting organizations have the same editorial slant as the American media. The weekly Der Spiegel (Germany), Economist and Daily Mirror (U.K.,) and Le Monde (France) are all leftward leaning, accounting for a majority of of the newspaper circulation in Europe.

<u>View of Government</u>

There is a massive gulf between how a national government is viewed by the United States and the rest of the world. Most people outside the U.S. have been conditioned to view a national government as a pro-active entity that actively serves the interest of the country, doling out favors and benefits to their maximum limits. The U.S. was founded on the belief that a central government should not be trusted and that citizens and states bear the brunt of governing themselves together with arming itself with a strong militia. Most of the world bristles when conservatives and Republicans espouse smaller governments and when the U.S. flexes their military muscle.

<u>Resentment of Caucasian civilization</u>

Ironically, Europeans lead the charge that Western civilization has a lot to do with past and present ills. They contend that White Europeans like Christopher Columbus caused widespread pestilence and annihilation in Central America. In general, liberal conventional wisdom states that white males have generally been the cause of the deconstruction of the civilized world especially with their generally cruel treatment of minorities, women, children and the working class. This explains why Western Europe is trapped in a Muslim quandary. They are being incessantly infiltrated by radical Muslims and are caught between securing their borders and allowing the occasional terrorist attacks in their big cities. The only country to attempt to secure its border Britain, has been subject to worldwide international scorn for allowing *Brexit*, its exit from the European Union.

Chapter Seven: Who Becomes a Politician?

Being a successful politician requires a combination of the following assets and characteristics: charisma, knowledge, persistence, a sense of sacrifice, empathy, ruthlessness, connections, confidence, honesty, empathy, integrity, and caring. Credentials and character traits are observable and verifiable, but what is more absorbing and interesting are the motivations behind running for political office.

It is difficult to generalize what makes a politician run for office because every politician is his or her unique person with their own set of personality quirks and tendencies. However, the motivations for running for political office can be reduced to a precious few.

<u>Serving constituents</u>

In the U.S., the first congressmen and senators treated their jobs as something that they simply needed to do as part of their patriotic duty. They treated their original occupations as their primary trade and the job of serving in Congress was a far second. After Congress adjourned, they were all eager to return to their jobs a lawyers, farmers, ministers, businessmen, teachers, or whatever their trade or occupation was. This was in line with the Founding Fathers' disdain for politics, especially politics coming from a central government. To the first editions of national politicians, legislating was a chore that was necessary for the sake of the country even if it meant that their normal lives would be disrupted.

This all seemed to change by the end of the 19th century when the seat of government was firmly entrenched in Washington, D.C. Ironically, as their constituencies got bigger legislators spent more time in Washington, D.C. instead of in the local districts and states that they represented. Legislating was quickly becoming their full-time job as the spent the time between congressional sessions campaigning for re-election – they were full time politicians who were either in office or running for office.

Today most politicians in the do not run for U.S. Congress or the U.S. Senate right away except for some few exceptions. Most full-time politicians get their start at the local level – city councilmen is the most common starting position – and accumulate the credentials and support that they need if they want to aspire for higher office in the future. There is a famous saying that "all politics is local," especially true when someone is just starting out on a journey for political career.

A neophyte politician starts out in his town looking for the lowest level of office the concerns and issues seem mundane. It could be getting a pothole fixed or repainting street signs – seemingly little unimportant matters. But as one's political career progresses the issues become more complex and weightier often involving thousands of people and lots of money. When we talk about the President of the United States, we are up to dealing the billions of people and trillions of dollars at stake. A congressman or senator may want an airplane manufacturing facility built in a city in his state or a president may want to fire missiles at a belligerent enemy country. The stakes just get bigger.

<u>Sense of public service</u>

Military servicemen and police have a sense of duty that makes them put their lives on the line in the name of service to the public. Many politicians actually have come from the military and police ranks - over a dozen U.S. presidents saw action in battle and were even wounded fighting for their country. And while it doesn't appear that any U.S Presidents were former police officers, many police officers became mayors, congressmen, and governors.

Sense of service comes from a willingness to sacrifice part of one's self to serve others and many politicians undoubtedly possess this quality.

<u>Power</u>

Power and political office have been intertwined since homo sapiens stood upright and figured out that they needed to get along with other people. It is the nature of man to have power and to crave for dominion over other men. There is a variety of reasons for seeking power, all of them interrelated.

First, it provides a feeling of authenticity because power provides those wielding it the freedom to live life the way they like. For them there with no need for pretense because they do not have to act the way people expect or want them to act.

Second, it provides a feeling of control. Having control provides freedom from dealing with the uncertainties from awaiting what others will do. For those with a particular ideology control over making sure that ideas and ideals are not compromised, control over how things are carried out, leading to control over the future outcomes. If one can control the factors that lead to future events, then power over the future is secured.   The most important aspect of this feeling of control is the feeling of control over other people. Controlling other people means controlling their behavior, and ultimately the outcomes of that their behavior will produce.

Third, power provides freedom – the freedom to do whatever, whenever, and wherever you want.

In politics just important as power itself are two issues: First, how the politician won his position of power in the first place and second, what happened to the politician after he or she assumed that power. There are people "destined" for power and many are blessed with being amiable, extroverted and agreeable. Charisma and charm count a lot in politics and many are able to capitalize on these. The past two Democrat presidents Barack Obama and Bill Clinton share these traits in abundance. They did well during their campaigns by seeming to be friendly and approachable. They can charm the pants off voters and their constituents and can make followers eat off their hands. Nice guys finish first and these two presidents certainly did.

Then there are those who won their positions through guile and even brute force.   Dictators in banana republics are perfect example as well as numerous coup d'etats all over the world.   Some say Donald Trump won the presidency in fashion - he bullied his Republican counterparts in the primary elections and may even have colluded with Russia to "steal" the elections from Hillary Clinton.

The second issue is what happens to politicians after they achieve power. A precious few become better leaders aa they "grew" into their position such as the cases of Ulysses S. Grant, Abraham Lincoln, and Harry Truman. Most simply coast as they leave the presidency as practically the same person come out. And then there are others who somehow let the power swallow their better selves as with Republican Richard Nixon in the Watergate scandal and the sexual hi-jinks that Bill Clinton had in the White House with Monica Lewinsky.

<u>Money?</u>

In modern times, it may be difficult to find a politician who used national or state office to financially profit as a result of their position. The most recent convicted high-profile miscreant is Democrat Rod Blagojevich of Illinois who was sentenced to fourteen years in prison in 2012 because he apparently caused others to gain financially while he was governor of Illinois, although he himself did not profit personally.

It is difficult for a politician to earn a fortune while in office. For this reason, most U.S. congressmen and senators run for and win positions after they have accumulated a large enough pool of assets. Living in Washington, D.C. is an expensive proposition and even to just maintain a house in the area can be prohibitive.

Most politicians begin earning serious money AFTER they leave office. Some take high executive positions in large companies that value a politician's name, which can add heft and prominence to a company. A politician can also start a new life as an expensive "consultant" or lobbyist and is able to millions of dollars so that he can use his connections to help various enterprises and individuals influence legislation. Some will write best-selling memoirs and exposes'. Ex-presidents earn millions of dollars in speeches and appearance fees, ensuring a steady stream of income post-White House.

<u>A special note on candidates running for national office</u>

But a person running for the highest positions in U.S. government including senators from large states, the Vice-President, and President, appears to demand many character and personality qualities that could make a psychiatrist cringe. A run for national office takes all the motivations we described earlier and infuses them with extra doses of vanity, insanity, superhuman effort, thick skin, cruelty, recklessness and irrational behavior. After all seeking office requires setting aside part of one's humanity. There are good and bad days – usually extremely long ones that can wring the emotions out of mere mortals. Still they aren't "allowed" to be show genuine anger, sadness, or elation and cannot come across as being bummed out, impatient, and surly.

Whether they come out losers or winners is beside the point. What is ultimately more interesting is how the process changes them. Ultimately the question arises: are they in it for themselves or do they really want to serve the public?

Conclusion: The Country's Best Interests? Or Theirs?

<u>When presidents became suspects</u>

Television and the Vietnam War probably started the U.S. down the path of politicians being untrustworthy. The Vietnam War was the first major international affair that was covered extensively by the three major media outlets then: print, radio, and especially television. Determined and audacious reporters risked their lives to show the gulf between what the U.S. generals were saying about the war and what was actually happening on the ground. When President Johnson parroted the reports of his generals, he might as well have been making bald-faced to Americans about the realities of the war. The U.S. public suspected that at the very least, their Commander-In-Chief allowed himself to be misled by his armed forces or at worst was lying bald-faced to his countrymen.

Johnson's furtiveness and deceit overwhelmed the groundbreaking programs on civil rights and welfare that he pushed through. He could not even make it past his own party's nominating process and walked away from re-election in 1968.

Less than a decade later Richard Nixon was caught in his own web of deceit and lying, electing to cover-up the spying shenanigans of Republican campaign operatives instead of being honest with the American public. It did not matter a whit that Nixon opened up China to the world or that he started the exit from the Vietnam War. The bad simply far outweighed the good.

More than anyone else, the two men led the country down the path of suspicion being the default state of the American public towards its major institutions, and especially the political ones. Recessions, failed military operations, business failures, and even natural disasters were being blamed on politicians especially presidents.   Did the Bushes really want war to enrich their military/industrial friends? Did the Clintons really allow communist countries to steal valuable military and industrial secrets?

<u>The difficulty of assessing good intentions</u>

With some understanding of the motivations that we have examined in the previous chapter, we have a good window into the soul of politicians' past and present. Based on their accomplishments (or in some cases lack of accomplishments) we can have a pretty solid understanding of whether politicians generally work for the country's best interests or use their office to further their own or those of their friends.

In the U.S. The question of whether politicians use their office for personal gain or for service to the nation is usually not an easy one to answer. If sitting politicians were asked that question directly, Americans have been so jaded as to politicians' honesty that they would not believe or accept the answers anyway. And yet if we try to figure it out ourselves there are some roadblocks that are strewn along the way.

The problem in trying to determine whether a politician is acting in the best interests is because the observers' perceptions have been tinged with bias and preconceptions. In the U.S. a political observer's vision of proper governance as been reduced to two diametrically opposed political philosophies: liberal and conservative. Favoring one "side" or the other can render a particular event, piece of legislation, or presidential directive as "controversial" depending on which side of the political fence a person is on. In Chapter Five, several issues were discussed that has made it patently clear that a politician can be seen as right or wrong acting on one issue – it just depends on which political lenses are being worn.

For example, when George W. Bush ordered the invasion of Iraq his doubters claimed that he was doing it to enrich his friends in Halliburton of which his Vice-President Dick Cheney used to be the CEO. Bush supporters on the other hand believed that in trying to capture the Iraq dictator Saddam Hussein, he had the interests of Americans and the world because he was removing a major source of terrorism in the world.

On the flipside when Barack Obama led the passage of the Affordable Care Act (Obamacare) his supporters gushed that we had the best interests of Americans in mind because he wanted everyone to enjoy health care. His detractors warned and correctly predicted that Obamacare would eventually drive up premiums for private plans, make some insurers leave the healthcare marketplace altogether and make it more expensive for people to pay for their healthcare (you are penalized if you are not insured by any health plan). They say his universal healthcare program was but a vanity play to help secure his place in history.

Once in a rare while, politician doesn't even have to do anything because sometimes all he or she needs is show up -like Donald Trump. When he announced his candidacy for the U.S. presidency, a majority of Americans decided that he was simply an entertainment buffoon entering the race tp service his already inflated ego. As he progressed in the electoral process perceptions about Trump morphed – he wanted to use the office of the U.S. President to enrich himself and his family further. As a sitting president it doesn't seem to matter what Trump does or does not do, his reputation precedes him and there is no way that he convince his many detractors that his motives are honorable. When critics are asked why they don't like him as a president, they hardly mention any specific policies that causes their disgust for Trump – they simply don't like him and that's all there is to it.

It is unfortunate that after over two hundred years as a nation, the common political landscape that liberals and conservatives can congregate in and have civil and intelligent debate has just gotten smaller and smaller: You are either for the Second Amendment or for banning guns. You are either for abortion or against abortion. If you favor tax cuts for the rich then you must be a mean heartless capitalist. And so on.

In the beginning of the Republic, there was only one enemy: England. The major domestic issues were how to put food on every table and to protect citizens from harm. When+ the country was well into the 19th century slavery became the biggest enemy. As the country entered the 20th century foreign enemies came into the picture: Germany, Japan, and Russia. In the 1950's the enemy was communism and the countries that supported them. Then things went south from a civility standpoint.

In the last fifty years, Americans have found new enemies: each other. A big factor contributing to this is the tension brought about by concept of enforcing all manner of "rights" that we talked about in Chapters 4 and 5. So much focus has been put on rights over the past fifty years that very little emphasis has been placed on "obligations." For example, many parents have declared that they have the "right" to choose which school their fifth-grader should go to, while ignoring that the voucher that they will use is paid for by taxpayer dollars and funded by tax revenue the district that they live in. Or an employee can demand that she has the "right" to a living wage ignoring the fact that the employer who paid her living wage had to lay off another person so that he could afford the government-dictated wage.

As deep trenches have been created between both political philosophies over the past few decades, the tenor of the arguments between the liberal and conservative sides have become more acrimonious and combative. Supreme Court nominee confirmations are especially testy because a Supreme Court Justice can swing the "moral" direction of a country in a single vote. Opponents to a Supreme Court nomination will often hire third party investigators just to be able to dig up some dirt on the nominee. This standard methodology when candidates perform "opposition research" on their political opponents while running for office is now being done on judicial candidates

<u>Is U.S. politics all bad and are politicians really that selfish</u>

The Founding Fathers and the institutions they have built, especially the political ones, have turned the United States into the world's pre-eminent superpower in both a military and economic aspect – it boasts the biggest defense force and the biggest Gross Domestic Product on the planet. A vast majority of scientific, medical, and technological developments over the past one hundred years or so have come from the United States. There is no place on earth where the descendants of former African slaves brought to predominantly Caucasian countries have become billionaires, chief executives, and even president as in the case of Barack Obama. Yet African-Americans continue to complain about the racist culture that is the U.S. and agitate for more "rights."

In their groundbreaking book, *Why Nations Fail,* the authors James A. Robinson and Daron Acemoglu show that a nation's success or failure does not depend on cultural factors, climate, geography, or religion but mostly by the political institutions that are established in their country. A lot can therefore be said about what kind of political institutions were built by the Founding Fathers of the country, and about warring politicians in the present who somehow have made things seem to work despite all the recent bickering.

Because of the groundwork for the political institutions that they created, the nation that is the United States has succeeded probably beyond the wildest dreams of every Founding Father and signer of the Declaration of Independence in 1776. Whatever the motivations of politicians are over the past two and half centuries, the collective polity that is the United States seems to be doing just fine.

I hope this book was able to give you some insightful information on politics and U.S. politicians.

Finally, if you enjoyed this book, then I'd like to ask you for a favor, would you be kind enough to leave a review for this book on Amazon? It'd be greatly appreciated!

Thank you!

www.ingramcontent.com/pod-product-compliance
Lightning Source LLC
Chambersburg PA
CBHW040239240726
48664CB00001B/201